THE PILGRIM'S TRAIL

FRANCES SPURRIER

Best wishes,
Frances

Published by Cinnamon Press
Meirion House,
Glan yr afon,
Tanygrisiau
Blaenau Ffestiniog,
Gwynedd, LL41 3SU
www.cinnamonpress.com

ISBN: 978-1-909077-38-6

British Library Cataloguing in Publication Data. A CIP record for this book can be obtained from the British Library.

Designed and typeset in Palatino by Cinnamon Press
Cover from original artwork 'Cwm Idwal' by Simon Whitehouse, © Agency: Dreamstime.com
Cover design by Jan Fortune

Printed in Poland

Cinnamon Press is represented in the UK by Inpress Ltd www.inpressbooks.co.uk and in Wales by the Welsh Books Council www.cllc.org.uk

Acknowledgments

Some of these poems have previously appeared in *Tears in the Fence, South, HQ, 14, Staple* and *Reach.* The poem 'Living with Cleopatra' originally appeared on the website Nthpostition. Other poems have been anthologised in *Reaching Out* (Cinnamon Press, 2013) and 'Gospel Pass' appears in *The Poet's Quest for God* (Eyewear Publishing, 2014). Many of the poems which appear in this book formed part of a prize winning submission in the Cinnamon Press Collection competition. Acknowledgements are due to the editors of these publications.

Many colleagues and friends have helped shape my writing and thinking about poetry. My thanks are due to them all. In particular, I would like to thank Fiona Sampson at the Roehampton Poetry Centre, Siobhan Campbell at Kingston University, Jan Fortune at Cinnamon Press and Mike Loveday.

Love and gratitude to Neil for patience and proof-reading.

Contents

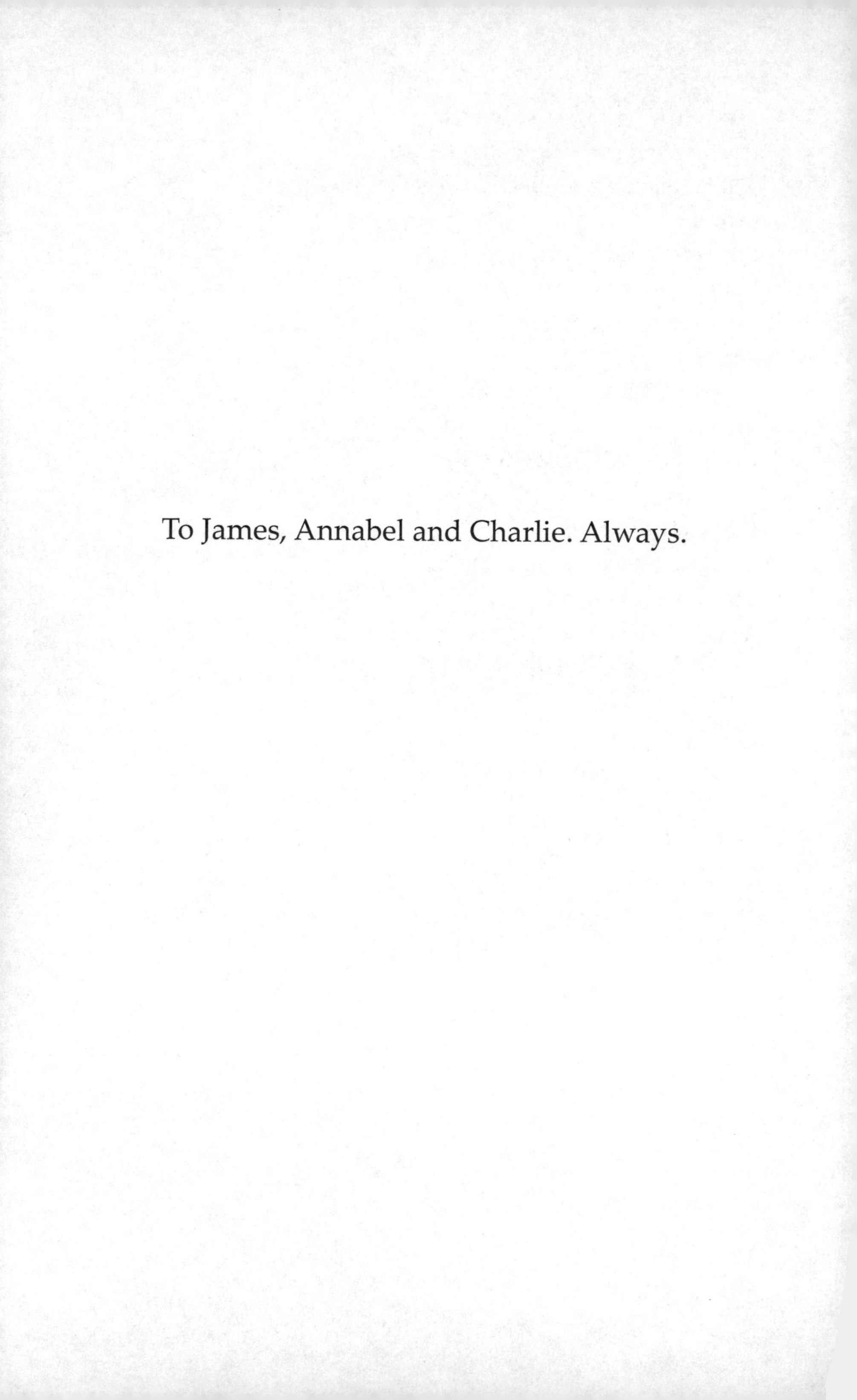

To James, Annabel and Charlie. Always.

The Pilgrim's Trail

Long and long has the grass been growing,
Long and long has the rain been falling,
Long has the globe been rolling round.

Walt Whitman

Radiocarbon dating

Carved in cellular streams
by the hand of one deity or another
we were born.

We burned away the dark;
drew the first music from the first strings
beneath blackened oak.

The sea inscribed our history on a palimpsest of sand
then erased it.

We forged iron. Harrowed the ground for ideas,
or angels, or ideas of angels.

Flowers conjoined the earth to the air —
received the comfort of morning —
and nothing dwelled beneath
that we knew.

If you should worry about us
alone in the short dawn,
we have left writings for you
drawn with a stick
in the dust of our souls' leavings.

Somehow we found the words.

Sea Level

Further than history, the legends thicken...
George McKay Brown Song: Further than Hoy

Five a.m. A chill light settles over the dark of the sea,
winds are light to moderate as I set out in my boat.
We leave behind the suck and clutch of sand.
Every damned tern and kittiwake arrives to scream us away
from the witch-haunted shore, where, as a child,
I gathered whelks
with my brothers teasing. We sharpened knives,
fought for crabs in buckets. A haul of memories nets itself,
lands thrashing on the deck.
The engine sounds its low, faithful beat.
The boat shudders through, shawled in a cold mist.

Beyond the catch I have no interest in fish.
The churchyard is full of names, there are many ways to join
them:
fishing is one, drinking another, mourning a third.
I fish, I drink, I mourn, yet I am trying not to add my name
to that eternity.
I stand like an effigy on deck, my coffee already cold
the fog-muffled bells sound out, the beacon lances early light.
I look back at the Church cross on Green Holm
see the shape of prayer and suffering,
feel I've had my fill of those.

I am alert for seals! Wary too. For if they suspect you of spying
they will double their disguise and dive beneath the oily waves.
As members of old sea tribes, we have much in common
searching for where salt won't rake the skin
nor wind howl sleep from shrinking bodies.

Scene by the River

The vodka stains the light with a translucent guilt.
Here in this city of rags and rage, beside the Thames,
it is time to acknowledge the screaming gulls
inside our heads. The river is swollen with rain,
flowing so fast even the swans are turning circles,
paddling without purpose in the reckless current.

I bet you thought the prayers were all for you
just because that's how it began, in some garden
with damson and apple where the sundial
had no hours to measure.

Does time pass if there are none to notice?
Yes. And here we are in the yellowing dusk of Autumn.
Lights blink fondly at one another from across the bank
like lamps lit in a whore's window.

Selkie

i

Drunk on cheap whisky from the Institute, I first met Megan.
I told her I was a poet.
After the fourth scotch, I told her I was a shepherd.
after the fifth that I was thinking of becoming a monk.
A whisky monk? she said, then caught my hand
and we tore around to the sound of flute and fiddle.
She told me she was a Selkie, changed to a woman
                    to trap a fisherman.
We laughed so much, tumbled out into the cold wet wind
staggered about the shoreline, sobered up only when twelve
                    drifting lights at sea
reminded us we were alone in that salt-sheet night.

I kept her skin in a wooden chest, and hid the key,
                    day and night.
It worked for a while.
My Megan. She laughed a lot in the early years
wove nets like the other women, made passable butter
salted away beef in brine, or maybe barrels of tears.
We had two children, a boy and a girl
they ran naked and shouting on the shore;
Megan swam every morning, summer and winter
but the children were forbidden the water.

ii

Another fruitless search.
I unlatch the wind-battered door, retreat past the sorrow
of empty chairs, head straight for a drink,
turn up the radio, drown the silence.
A boy and girl there'd been in this cottage of stone,
a man and wife, but now I am alone.

I fall into disorderly sleep;
outside the wind tears slate from roof and washing from lines
puts the whole world in a rage.
Suddenly she's here dripping seawater on bare boards.
I am calm enough, in that hinterland of a waking dream.
I take down the lantern,
think nothing of trailing my beloved ghost into the storm's rage,
for none of this is real.
We snake down the cliff path, the sea lashes at the rocks
carves the cliff to memorial stone beneath my feet.
The lighthouse flashes in its interrupted code: lament, loss.

Hidden in a cave, I find them,
playing to the music of thunderous seasounds —
ivory combs, a whale's tooth and a tin of marbles.
This half-home for a seachild
graced with electric blue algae, decked with shells.

My daughter is sixteen now.
She takes long, lonely walks on the shoreline
tries to capture in paint the texture of reflected water,
the opacity of lapis lazuli, but is never happy with the result.
She waits for me to return from my sea- trips;
they are fewer and fewer, the catch scarce.

But it is my boy I am most proud of.
He works in the city, cares nothing at all for fishing.

Swan in the Graveyard

The service washed you with a cloth of light
a vision already yours, granted to others.

Behind you in the autumn dawn
the river misted like firesmoke.

Tinnitus

Imagine that, sleepless!
Marbles in a tin bucket;
crashing in a meteor sky.

When the sea turns upright
persuaded by gravity
to wash down the moon,
craters of grit will descend
and the new seas – the moon seas
empty out.

Slipways

October 27th, 1962 The Cuban Missile Crisis

Between an old chair vacated by the River Severn,
and the mud flats and salt marshes of Tites Point,
our house lies, a wobbling-white cottage on the slipway
where the ferry once ran from Wales to the mainland.

We live, Aunt Sofie, me — left in situ by my absent mother —
plants, cats, chickens, in a tense cohabitation, an opaque life
like muddied water. Elsewhere the USA and Russia stir molten
lava on a lethal stove. Here at home we bake and bicker.

I'm late! I fail at the chores I am set, it is my turn to clear.
Who pays for the clothes on my back, the food I eat?
Aged nine, the sin of pride already mine. Missiles of spite
are fired point blank along the mud-sucking estuary shallows

where geese argue and shout and I shout back.
I walk home from school through the cemetery for a dare.
I don't care. If the dead lie beneath my tread
I know nothing of it, nor do the dead know of me,

or how their numbers will soon increase
and this time there will be no graves, no white markers,
nothing to show how the call of history is drowned
in a clatter of pans.

Patricio

Memory is an old farmhouse poised
on its half-bred mountain,
prone to winter's damage
and the soul's dark.
Look out at night
through icy glass
the view is the same:
          sheep withered grass,
          a small stone church
where legends thick as hogweed
          choke the roof,
          and sunrise halts the damp — momentarily.
Sunrise is a wanderer on the hill,
anxious,
following paths the otter
made in sleep and sudden waking.
These are the ley lines of lean years
          scratched in tumbling scree,
          a trace of ancient causes unresolved.

In Memoriam

Past the sullen river and a patch of parkland garden
the trail we all followed, round and round;
the same few friends leaving home in sunlight or in snow.
Winter is long, but winter always turns to Spring.
When trees give leaf
    salute their branches over the places where you walked
    and the dogs have played out their games
then we will have
    all we are entitled to ask.
The earth will remember your tread
sincerely, and with grace,
will send back its light with strength to spare
for those of who wait behind
last year's rosehips frozen over on the rose.

What finished the Romans in Britain

Dividing the country surgically
at its narrowest point
was the easier thing to do
for sublime engineers of straight lines,
less of a problem
than coining Welsh gold and squabbling
with Scotts or Saxons
like gulls over fishbones.

It was always too cold.

Hadrian divided mud
even as the land
entered its first summer.

Cuthbert loses his cool

Cuthbert is cross.
Usually he is a man of devout habits and even temper
(after all he will be a Saint).

But today the ravens are driving him crazy.
Just this morning they tore the thatch from his roof
despite requests to stop.

Admittedly not much of a roof, but it's his roof,
and he needs it,
            to keep dry while at prayers.
            to stop the lapis lazuli running
on the Lindisfarne Gospels.

His needs are few but he does like a roof.
Lord! Spare him these ravens.
They understand nothing.

The Pilgrim's Trail

Of the nights, the last had been the coldest. No-one slept.
Aidan has crossed the rough seas from Iona,
rested at Aberlady, now on foot
with boots of skin, cross and torch
he goes to found a monastery.
past cliffs of chalk and flint,
counterpoint of day and night.

In the beginning was the word.
Heaven itself has sent him phrases
They appear in his mind without inducement,
as markers by which he orients himself.
Simple stories. Parables. Miracles.

Over a narrow sky cloud strips are thinly pared.
The isle alternates. Sometimes land. Sometimes afloat
crossing the sands he can hear the sea following him
breakers echo each other
try to out-clamour the birds.
Around are piers of shallow chalk, wide bays of flint,
shifting dunes and marram grass.

It takes two hours to cross.
Footprints sink like ghost lines in blue and shining sand.
Distance stretched, time compressed
but unity remains.
See! The ground is covered in signatures.
The tide creeps inexorably over the trail
hiding the paths to real places.
He will build a causeway
that all may pass.

Gospel Pass

To Bianca

High where the rain is glass
and the sky overburdened with cloud,
Gospel Pass
        winds its way
                through the black hills of Wales.

The crusaders passed this way, they say
resting the rough wooden cross against a rock
as they carried it
from Llanthony Priory to Hay
or offered it up at Capel-y-Ffin.

I will lift up mine eyes
There are places where you don't want to look down.
There are places where you don't want to leave
yet leave you always do
while the mountain batters
        with its hailstorm breath
        renders inarticulate
a heart as sound as stone.

Aberfan

Even half-way up the view was coal-black.
Black as winter which hung in the sky
over chapels and song books
over trees and telegraph poles
over terraces of brick, row on row
over the day we woke up with a clear feeling
that the hills were hollow
that we had made our valleys and towns,
but didn't believe in fragility.

Nothing in the song-books
told us the landscape could one day fold up,
slip away,
turn to ashes of roses.
We made the hollow hills
with their unspent jurisdiction.
We knew all we had made could be unmade,
but we chose not to believe.

Commercial Road

There were low coal stocks and strikes
so freezing was a full time occupation for a woman.
Men built the cages which filled the pits
which mined the coal which heated the homes
and drove the turbines which fired the steel
which made the frame which support the house that Jack built.
But what did the girls do?
The end of the shift is the end of the shift and the girls
are in trouble again with hair the texture of sherbet lemons,
Ferry Cross the Mersey and the last train home at ten.

Jam

Ten-thousand days she had planned,
but spent them walking the same street;
emptying the bins. Brought up a daughter
and two sons, fed the cat - this cat or a different one.
A generic cat, Maisie or Daisy; a thin scrap of black and white fur,
curled in a space, asleep in the no-light time.

She has baked a Victoria sponge
It lies there, leaking onto the plate.

Home

Outside the train the landscape speeds up.
Through the tunnel my blunt white face flashes
back from walls, from fields of yellow rape.
        Crosskeys to Abertawe.
        Casnewydd strangled by twists of new road,
roads taken or not taken
an ill-drawn town no-one saved.

The moon is an orange hanging
        over Twm Barlwm:
terraces cling to the foot of the hill.
Two children sleep in a house beneath.

A woman in a Fifties coat
makes a brief appearance on a platform.
Water creeps over the high heels of her shoes;
her feet are drowning.
        If she leaves the dress shop,
                she leaves
the false smiles in the photographs
                                the home where two children sleep.

Y Fenni. Yes, I remember the name although we never used it.
A young man sits opposite me
pleased with the shine of his untried boots,
he can see his face in them. He looks like my son.
He looks as though be believes in a way back.

Out of Seahouses

Stand knee deep at low, numbing water
to gather prawns and winkles.
On reflection, the sea is a vast accumulation of tears.

Five boats are left
to fish from these shores.

Lime Kilns over Conistone

From origin to edifice – our past is all that we remember of the weeping dead. Lime kilns make mortar –
    quicklime slaked with water
    mortar for sheep-sheltering walls
    mortar to hang a wall around a man-made summit.

Beyond the one you think you can see.

Walk for hours with burning feet
and your eyes fixed on a far point,
like the future, it will not come any closer.
Or else it is suddenly upon you, diminished.

Groves of tumbled stones are shelter turned headstone
empty cloisters of the hills,
    oblivious to the gale's edge.

Communion

Little girls drift by in white dresses,
clutching at glasses of lime juice
served by nuns; good-tempered, smiling.
Hail Mary, full of grace.

We are not allowed on the lawn.
Non-communicants. Small zionist infiltrators
in a world of incense and Latin prayer.
The shaded garden behind the Convent
lies like a green oasis beyond
the playground's dusty desert.

One of the nuns watches me watching.
Would you like one? she asks,
offering a tin of biscuits over the wall.
I meet her gaze unsmiling, rosary beads
hidden under blue serge.

Headscarves

The magic chime of midnight
turns the mind to pumpkins;
I lose the faculty for decoding secrets through a blue screen.
My mother enters,
she has come to breathe the air of expressions.

When she died we found
old headscarves, silk reliquaries outside of place and time
the promised land uncharted.

It rained the day we emptied out the house but the rain was not
discouraged from impressing its grief on scoured glass.

My father does not appear.
Too much melodrama for his austere tastes.

Warsaw Wedding

We dance on the deep carpets
of an expensive hotel, yards
from the site of the ghetto.

Under a summercloud sky
the bride's roses drift in hair and bouquet;
the hands of the clock move slowly.
You and I, forgotten guests
seated at a table
beyond the reach of cake and speeches.

May you always be like this
frozen in white rosebuds …
may you stay ....

What Tom said to the Witch

In addition to waking the dead
she offers readings; crystal globes, tea leaves.
You name it

the witch says, opening a leather bound ledger
of chants and incantations.
Price on application.

Fulfilling unkept promises is extra,
she informs the queue of grieving spirits
who creep nearby

hoping for salvation and settled debts,
while she checks her varnished nails
for chips.

One frosty morning, as the witch
opened her sash window
to free an owl,

Tom took his opportunity, jumped the queue,
flew in to seek her help
with a gift

(... an ivory comb and a silver ribbon
for his Mother's
birthday)

The passing on of gifts is extra, snapped the witch,
brushing owlfeathers
from her Givenchy dress.

Tom had no money as the witch
well knew, but he held one ace
up his sleeve.

With stage whispers and many sighs
he called upon Hera
to intervene.

Hera? the witch interrupted,
turning green, what about Hera?
She shifted from foot to foot,

ghastly visions of one thousand years
imprisoned in a tree bole
for breach of the code.

She once met my mother in a fable, Tom replied.
Now it was his turn
to examine his nails.

File Retrieval

Turn away from the window,
you , Lady of Shalott, half-sick of shadows
uncover your eyes and stare back
    at the mirror.
Turn away from the arched window
the paraphernalia of weaving, all the believing, the unbelieving
    the passages of want.

Turn away from death. He was here yesterday
looking over your shoulder, tapping at the keyboard
    with skeletal fingers, planting messages on the screen
    about loving and dying
And if we could not stop for him, it was no problem at all
he said kindly.

Love Gothic Style

The air is pierced with half heard greetings
and a sense of you in the room,
        unsatisfied.
You did not leave then, or could not?

Some things lie unspoken in the dark
after day has ended
        and some things lie beneath black beams
        torn from the hall house
        behind the broken rose arch.

There in the cavernous kitchen
unrequited love hangs like meat from a meathook.

The importance of boats and rainbows in exceptional circumstances ...

This winter
gales peeled back our rooftop
like the lid from a can of sardines.
We rang the man to fix it
while the deluge poured
in with hilarity
over our carefully appointed plastic buckets
swishing, slopping
anointing what used to be the floor.
        Sorry, was this your house?
        You should have said before.

Somehow we were surprised when the sea tested our defences
and found us powerless.

We rowed boats up country lanes, parked cars in the trees.
This winter we needed a new Ark
Or for God to remember His pledge;
        take the rainbows out of storage.

The Golem of Old Prague

From the mud of the Vltava River he rose
the legend says, manlike, mystical
a creature of Kabbalistic prayer
    unleashed in torchlight.
    Yossel the Golem of Old Prague.
He was created they told him
to serve the Rabbi and community;
to obey not to distinguish
to live in a house, perform only the given tasks.

But it was harder than he thought to be alone.
There were so many rules.
He must not be curious, and yet, he is:
He should not distinguish, and yet he does.
Why does the carp flap out its life on slimy cobbles?
(He threw it back in the river but still it died, foolish thing!)
What lies hidden beneath the upturned market stall?
How much water is enough to clean?
To drown?

It was harder than they thought to stop him.
The rabbi left his congregation in mid-prayer
to chant and re-chant the same lines
You will be there at Judgement Day, though in what form I cannot say.

Yossel the Golem of Old Prague
    his statue sanctified by shining armour,
    guardian of the gate of the ghetto of Josevov.
Behind him lie headstones like broken teeth in a space so scarce
barely a blade of grass fits between at the Old Jewish Cemetery.
Behind him lie, twelve deep, the dead of Bohemia and Moravia.

Hilchenbach, 1936

To my father

When you board this train, aged seventeen,
you will disappear to the life of an unknown city
a language never wholly learned
an accent always retained in
the dark recesses of the throat.
You will not hear the screech of wheels
nor feel the choking breath
from that other train as it pulls away
from a snowbound platform at Siegen.

All your life you will stand on a platform
knowing the past can have no other trace;
hearing the stink of that Siegen train
seeing it shrink, always
though it cannot be swallowed
by any kind of mist, can never vanish.

Thought-weeds

My friend, it was never likely that we would meet again
in the ruck and press of the London Underground,
between Bakerloo and heaven knows where;

or images from forty-odd years roll back
to find us gaping like actors startled by an early curtain.
What caused this action replay?

A picture of your brother – a poster
in a tube station announcing his sixtieth birthday.

Picture it! You attending this celebration
flanked by a muse, grown children, a minder or two,
as I kneel in my garden pushing weeds back into the earth.

Images of the great and the good line the tube walls.

Final Sentence

A father tries to enforce a contact order against his ex-wife to see his little daughter.

Each day fills with new grievance
in these years we do not have
in this house of no doors.

I kept one pair of my daughter's shoes;
shoes for a child of magic. Witch's child.

No power to leave them on the doorstep
at the stroke of midnight.
Lying tongues and loopholes.
Shoes cannot simply vanish.

The mind says you too are human
but the mind forgets
bedded down in its bitter song.

Sofia in the Garden of Hours at the Villa San Remigio

Destiny stopped him at this spot, grandfather Browne,
caught in Italy with broken wheel and stumbling horse
his carriage toppled in the dark cypress shade.

And so he stayed, and next to a thousand-year-old church
built a villa from fine white stone and called it San Remigio.
Crumbling now. But, Silvio, were we ever young?
The garden that we built remains, it shines in Spring
          with the sadness of new leaf.

Sometimes a guide stumbles past with his group of visitors
his voice a shallow pool reflecting mumbles of bright mosaics.
He tells them our story in waterfall hedges of box and yew
          in sculpted shapes of blindness.

The return of Mrs. Odysseus

She's been here years,
her distant stare
sharing the space with mice. Waiting is something
she knows more about than any other woman.

She is the leader of wives of absent heroes,
or a stonecast version,
living in a subterranean maze
encased in her name, Penelope.

You meet here there
beneath the tourist run of the great house
where room guides chant assignations and catholic purges,
where in dark passageways and vaulted cellars
abandoned statues lie.

As you beckon she unfolds herself, steps forward –
lifts the lifeless hem of her gown
takes the stairs two at a time.

No-one notices the return of Mrs Odysseus to the garden.
What's one more visionless beauty in so many?

Urns like redundant suitors line the driveway.
Deep within a pool glints the disembodied head of an angel.
It is May. Strange injurious plants thrive
but there are also blossoms.
She walks over crushed petals.
climbs upon the plinth vacated by the broken angel,
prepares for another millennium or two.

Soon a teacher forms a group of schoolchildren
around her feet. *Who's this*? they ask
Aphrodite the teacher confidently asserts.
Penelope resists the temptation to straighten her gown
rub one stone heel against the other. This new apotheosis suits.

The air smells of deadnettle, of blackthorn.
She is surprised at how much she misses
the sound of the sea.

Unexpected meeting in the Peggy Guggenheim Collection, Venice

We were standing in front of Picasso when you both arrived
unbidden from Oxfordshire, having escaped for a moment
the Alasdair Sawday guide and your place in it;
the rigid hospital corners of sheets and home-made preserves.

In Dorsoduro we landed half-awake – like snowy egrets
flown too far from usual tidal marshes –
yet glad of the chance to view a new but similarly
endangered species. Such surprises the maestro

himself could disguise in the dove grey markings of
of *La Baignade*. Or Jackson Pollock fluster
the confused viewer with his *Eyes in the Heat*.
But lacking their vision, I reach no conclusion about meetings.

A frail and wolfish moon shone over Venice
which you tried to film
from the crumbling balcony of a Palazzo,
overlooking the Grand Canal.

Pruning

after Ted Hughes, Wycoller Hall

August. Late evening. Across the park
the cedar of Lebanon is casting
shade on the lawn.

A house of rose-coloured stone
which has seen too many
wars. Too many worries.

Lovers arriving, lawyers leaving
deeds, griefs, gifts, graves;
a succession of ponies called Jasper.

Shades of servants long departed
scrawl lipstick messages
on attic walls

as if to remind themselves
of tasks
uncompleted.

The wisteria needs pruning.
If not done soon it will be too late.
And the jasmine.

I'm here, but nothing

I coat bodies in lemon drift
paint limbs in white lava, firebrick red.
I give you polka dot neutrinos and quarks, the infinity net
made from reflected light.
I ask only for an end to war.

I can see down through the hollow universe
that somewhere beyond matter there is raw power
that beyond the traffic lights on the corner
is a place where men keep hold of the dark.

Some see things differently. Some see nothing.
But let us not speak of the abyss; it is commonplace,
it is near - not even as far as the apple seller's cart.

Limehouse Blues

Having no taste for the journey back to Asia,
she stays to run a laundry, opens a story-teller's booth.

With salt-caked skin men reel up from docked ships,
scrofulous, their pockets full of coins,
searching for beer and lodging

Near the hounding beat of sawmills
and the stench of lead, they wait
for as long as it takes for her tale to start.

She rifles through testers and pillow slips
brought by maids from the big houses;
harangues boiling sheets with wooden tongs,
to proper cleanliness.

In a basement room, lit by a single oil lamp
where steam serves for breath. She
coughs opium, thinks silvered
thoughts of Canton, begins...

*

When in early summer
the river water rose and burst its banks
willows and bamboos submerged,
save for their tips bared to the moon
she tells of that tide and fullness of desire
of the master for the slave Su Yin.

We lived in a palace with high carved beams
where lillies like precious jewels grew among
the rocks, carp swam in pools
and trees bowed heavy with spring blossoms
before the rain and gales.

As a child I ran dressed in red-flowered trousers
and tiger-faced shoes
until my mother fell from favour
— some imagined misdemeanour —
and we both were given to a man,
a hut dweller,
sent in an ox-cart,
with a small dowry
retaining only two lacquered boxes of black, red and gold
together with brushed letters of gilt-ink on rice paper
bearing the symbols of happiness.

All was work—but not for him.
The man who once had worked at night
pulling heavy wagons of merchandise,
sat puffing at a pipe, spitting the ground
impatient as a sycthe
while we stooped stiffly
the fields flooded,
the young rice set.

We lived in a hut
beside the fields of the fallen hart,
a hunting ground
where bones lay
scorched beneath trees.

Days were weaving,
dyeing, days were fruit and threshing
storing reeds, silkworms to feed
the fleeting branches of mulberry.
Days were lungs cramped by millet dust
and clouds of locust.
We prayed for rain, for snow to fall.

Su Yin died in winter, as leaves were torn
          from the date trees.
I was sold on again
to a merchant from Shantung
who had gold to spare
and happened to be passing
but when the hour came to leave
they claimed I stared at them, with the sharp,
sad eyes of my dead Mother.

Having no taste for the journey back to Asia
she stays to run a laundry, opens a storyteller's booth.

Living with Cleopatra

Because your reflection
in the shop window mirrored your
regal air you thought you were a queen —
Egypt perhaps — dying in an anguish of love.
Lacking only an asp, a draped litter,
you stood dreaming at the bus stop
waiting for the number thirty-nine.

Upon such history must Caesar sleep
and Antony face eternity in a schoolroom.
But I was just the water carrier
who dropped the pitcher, and ran.

Urban Myth

Another day,
more lies about fresh starts
more chances to erase the past or bring it along;
she's already tired of the words, this twisted tongue.

The station lies so close the lines rake through her mind.
Behind her on the bed a man snores, his name a space
where explanations faltered, language died.

*

Streets
lie bleached under a fabric moon.
The cafe is open early or perhaps never closed,
a few men, drunk on last night's habits
reach for empty glasses.

Beyond the city a road drains away.
Urban fox slinks past hypermarkets,
          tattoo parlours, shuttered shops.

*

Graffiti is his world rewritten in car paint:
          taupe, viridian, carmine.
It galls to leave a patch of wall unmarked
so he paints clean through the back of his hand
hell's own canvas, an outpouring of anarchic energy.

*

Through some error or oversight ...

an oak tree
has turned to a stack of papers
then to manure
used to encourage the growth of some other tree
newer in its desire to be.

Our definition of tree-ness cannot waiver;
not as ultimate sign of forgiveness,
or unchanging marker.

We have burned ourselves at the stake of definitions
must edit and sub-edit our borderlands
write the same formula for anxiety:
like scientists chasing the God particle.

The map says North lies the vanishing point.
Here, but not here.

Letters

No emails will be found
in dusty attics, tied with ribbon.
Without wooden pews, where will be carved
the names of dead lovers?

And take the War Memorial

Well, someone did.
Metal thieves left wreaths of poppies lying beneath a blank space;
mined the bronze plaque from the Cenotaph
to melt into train rails, copper wires and pipes
electric cabling - even manhole covers

a poor rat must slink through its share of roofless sewer.

But now police are poised to catch these merchant dealers
of illicit steel with new lighting and a live web-cam

And so the plaque is back! A replacement hammered into being
with all the solemnity of remembrance
guarded by DNA intruder spray.

Breathe again, grieve again.

These are the ways we ascribe value
            to the names of the fallen ;

for our blood-red poppies and strange rituals against forgetting,
the way we offer up bronze and copper,
to young men spent so freely.

Q and A

The Lime trees survive,
the fate of the Ash is uncertain.
Shocked swans go hollering down the high street
where the Thames now flows.
The land is supplying answers to questions
no-one remembered to ask.

Elegy for Diabaig

i

Take the road from Torridon
through the clouds to the sea.
It will end in the crofting and the fishing,
in Diabaig, remote, grieving its loss
of souls.

Walking alone one black night
down by the little loch
my brother Murdo
swore he met a ghost
clad in Mackenzie tartan
who told him a dreadful secret
of clan treachery.

Murdo wept, invoked the Trinity,
drew a circle in the earth around his feet.
You cannot cross, he shouted
confusing belief with unbelief.

But then, it was New Year and Murdo liked his whisky.
Who does not have secrets and savage lessons
harpoon sharp to learn? Poor Murdo.
He'd only walked from Alligin to bring the mail;
died soon after, his tale unfinished.

I was the one who went to France. Dunkirk.
I was the one who fought to cross the magic circle
dressed in cloud tartan,
to solve the mystery
of belonging.

ii

Take the road from Torridon;
through the clouds to the sea.

Here in Diabaig, everything is more or less than this;
    piled creels on the quayside,
    burned ribs of a foundered skiff.
Everything is more or less than the last cottage,
red telephone box, old shop.

Quiet on the hillside in their circle of fallen stone
find three nameless graves.
Tenement of clay.
Find a rusted bicycle leaning, waiting.
The river is vast, swollen.
The trees have found their voice,
give leaf after the long winter.
And the sound of the river is the drum at the gate of thunder.

Knitting Sheep for a Living

During drought, 2013

Hell, I'm no gull, no wheeler-dealer on God's air currents.
I believe in human will.
Come buy my knitted sheep,
nice lady, come buy my sheep.

Dead lambs are the frozen gifts of this freak Spring
their tiny corpses, unsuckled;
baptism of ice, funeral rite, all one.

Spring will bring flood melt
and mud to drown in —
tractors stuck to the axles.

Come buy my knitted sheep,
nice lady, come buy my sheep.

Come by. The hills say scrape your boots on my face;
hide my tears in your constant rain.

The day we bought …

sunk my heels through a rotted floorboard;
dismayed the agent
light from the sun disarrayed your hair,
inveigled the dust from old curtains.
Pre-owned, pre-loved, pre-arranged.

The day we sold
          our youngest cried.

Caretakers only,
and lacking skill at that
what comfort could we offer?

Undone days
          like broken toys in a box
          too many,
 yet few enough.

You the Last Leper: Art installation on Spinalonga Island

I'm not sure how it's done.
Baking under the rock and the Cretan sun,
while a tunnel of mirrors
reflects back my peering face
in a sea of white crosses.
Media vita in morte sumus.
In the midst of life we are in death.

Above the ruined hospital and the old fort
a steel crucifix is hoisted.

If I'm the last leper, what should I believe?

I decide to believe:
that empty-eyed sockets of gun placements
are the need to defend made manifest;

that flags in the breeze are the black emblems
of disease;

that those who burn,
burn with those who came before;

that for Cretan, Venetian, Turk or tourist,
flesh torn on bare rock is all flesh.
And I believe
infinity is a trick of the light.

Love of a sort

Winter comes with a mute confession:
a clock's dull hands circle the hours
a ring of dust lies on the mantel.
The garden settles reluctantly under the first frost.

I have taken down my book, one of the few you didn't burn.
A letter falls to the floor. It is yours — unsigned.

From my chair I listen to the rooks
sing their way down river
        they count the years of our parting .

        What have I learned?
        That stains of bitterness are difficult to remove.

So I will press my palms together, bow to you in my dreams
as if we two were Japanese priests met to discuss the Sutras.

Epilogue

And at the end, the world is this.
Paradise and now.
I am not what you wanted.
Your grief is like a star or a naked stem
in a flower garden;
the grace of a lit window
against a dark façade.

Longing has left the garden.

Forgive me it is time,
the painful hour when I shall
sign this letter with crosses,
send flowers for your blue vase.

Resilience

i

Filtered through this grain of cloth
light of the menorah. Just
nine candles. Nine small flames
to regale the mind with unimaginable stories:
            crossing burning sand;
taking the last train to nowhere.
The choice which is no choice.
To stay? To wait? To pray?

To watch the candles diminish.

ii

Ephemeral these faces. Vision flares like grief,
eyes foxed by the first scarlet veins of the maple
before the fall from grace.
Among the cedar rays and dust motes of the living
the novice in a white gown
kneels before the window.
Before the prayer, before the oath
before the unction of forgiveness
come the words no-one can hear.

Today fire is on the heath
and the sky itself seems charred
with the nerve and fibre of being.
Tomorrow we will say
this has happened and the rain fell silent;
this has happened and we will go forward.

Frances Spurrier writes and reviews poetry. Frances achieved a distinction in the MFA in Creative Writing from Kingston University in 2012 where she also taught Creative Writing. She is currently a PhD candidate at Roehampton University writing on the theory of poetics. Frances grew up in South Wales but now lives in London with her family. She is Reviews Editor for the popular poetry website, Write Out Loud.

In her own work Spurrier experiments in the margins of memory, landscape and spirituality. *The Pilgrim's Trail* is her first collection.